THE POLITICS OF THE FAMILY

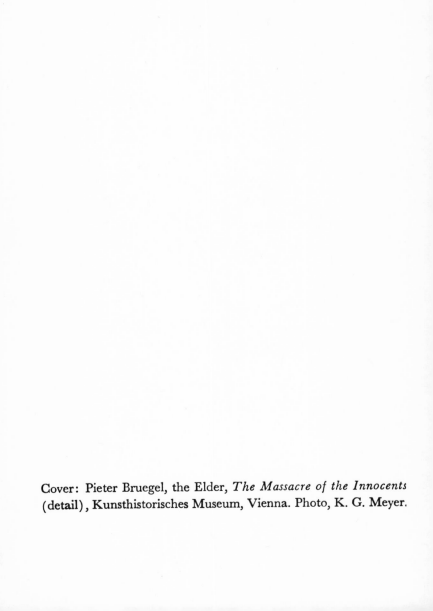

THE POLITICS
OF THE FAMILY

Massey Lectures, Eighth Series

by R. D. Laing

Canadian Broadcasting Corporation

Second impression 1969
Third impression 1970
Fourth impression 1971
Fifth impression 1972
Sixth impression 1973
Seventh impression 1974
Eighth impression 1974

ISBN 0-88794-028-5

Printed in Canada for
CBC PUBLICATIONS
BOX 500, STATION A, TORONTO   M5W 1E6
by The Hunter Rose Company

The five radio broadcasts published here were heard during November and December of 1968 as the eighth annual series of Massey Lectures. The 1968 Massey Lectures were arranged for broadcast by the *Ideas* unit of the CBC Department of Public Affairs, with Phyllis Webb as program organizer and production by Jeffrey Anderson in London. Begun in 1961 by the CBC to enable distinguished authorities in fields of general interest and importance to present the results of original study or research, the Lectures were named in honor of the late Rt. Hon. Vincent Massey, former Governor General of Canada.

RONALD DAVID LAING, 41, is a native of Glasgow, Scotland, where he attended grammar school and, in 1951, obtained his degree in medicine from Glasgow University. He also holds a Diploma in Psychiatric Medicine from the University of London, and received his psychoanalytical training between 1956 and 1960. Dr. Laing was a psychiatrist in the British Army from 1951 to 1953, then returned to Glasgow University to work in the Department of Psychological Medicine for three years. From 1956 to 1967 he worked at the Tavistock Clinic and the Tavistock Institute of Human Relations. In the latter part of that period he served as principal investigator of the Institute's Schizophrenia and Family Research Unit and conducted research as a Fellow of the Foundations Fund for Research in Psychiatry. From 1962 to 1965 he was director of the Langham Clinic for Psychotherapy, London. Since 1965, Dr. Laing has been working with the Philadelphia Association, London, and in private practice. He has also been a visiting consultant at mental health centres in Bethesda, Md., and in Boston. His work with the Philadelphia Association, of which he is chairman and a founder member, is an attempt to develop, with a number of his colleagues, a new strategy in terms of the relation of psychotic breakdown to family and social networks. This includes establishing places which are not hospitals, nursing homes, or hostels, but simply households where there is no treatment in any conventional sense. Rather, there is an attempt to create an ambience where people can work through inner involvements without drugs, etc. Other books by Dr. Laing are *The Self and Others, Reason and Violence* (with David Cooper), *The Families of Schizophrenics* (with Aaron Esterson), *Interpersonal Perception, The Divided Self,* and *The Politics of Experience & The Bird of Paradise.* He is also on the editorial board of a number of journals dealing with existential psychology and psychiatry.

In these talks I have sketched tentative outlines of some components of a prospective systematic theory that does not yet exist.

I have not presupposed in the listener or reader any knowledge of the work with families (therapy, research, theory) carried out, especially in the United States, in the last 25 years.

A list of the key people in this field, were it to include everyone, would be too long: and misleading, were I to mention the few who have especially influenced me. I have been influenced by some, primarily through their writings: others, by personal association and friendship: others indirectly, through their influences on others, etc. The reader new to this field, who wishes to follow through into the background of family studies of the kind from which these talks derive, can do so by looking up the footnoted references which, containing extensive bibliographies, are gate openers to the whole field.

I hope that my fellow "professionals" will find something to interest them here. The theory of sets and mappings is being applied to great effect in linguistics, kinship systems, mythology, and other areas of social science. Can we apply this way of thinking to "the psychosocial interior" of families in our own society? Definitely yes. But what will it yield? Will it be fruitful, will it enable us to discover more, see more clearly, understand better, provide useful and effective guidelines for therapy, help to get our research designs into sharper outline? We do not yet know. This might be a treacherous cul-de-sac. But I think the risk is worth taking. It may be a way out of the cul-de-sac in which, *especially*, some of the most technically best research in this field can get stuck. Just because it is careful, and meticulous, such research sometimes leads to a type of analysis of familial interactions, which returns findings that somehow continually never seem quite able to answer the questions we really want answered. We have taught ourselves that it is useless to ask questions, when we have no methodology to answer them. But, between the impossible and the trivial, there may be a way that is both feasible and significant. At any rate, I would like to be counted as still trying to find it.

I did not make it easy for the Canadian Broadcasting Corporation in preparing these talks. It is a pleasure to thank Phyllis Webb and Jeff Anderson of the Canadian Broadcasting Corporation for making everything as easy as possible for me at all times.

R. D. L.

London. January, 1969

THE POLITICS OF THE FAMILY

CONTENTS

The first family to interest me was my own. I still know less about it than I know about many other families. This is typical. Children are the last to be told what "really" was going on before they came into the world, especially when they want to know not merely a few discontinuous points in time, called dates, and other apparently "hard" facts, such as who was born when, died when, married whom, had what children, when, who earns what and how, and so forth.

I am concerned here with the texture of the actual lived experience of people in families: and with how the experience of people who live together is related to the dramatic structure, which is the social *product* of the interweaving of the lives of many people over many generations. It is remarkable that this dramatic structure, the very *product* of the interaction of the behaviour and experience of people, is, as a rule, not experienced by, and is unknown to, the very people who generate and perpetuate it.

In this type of inquiry the dates of public family events do not take us far. We must not ignore them, but we must not be deceived by them. Jack and Jill were married in 1960. There were over 100 wedding guests. Nevertheless Jack has never *felt* married to Jill, and Jill only began to feel "really" married to Jack some months after the wedding.

Although Jack has never felt married to Jill, he believes he is because he can remember going through a ceremony, that he knows is called a "marriage", and he has over 100 witnesses to prove it. But Jill is not satisfied. She does not want a pretence of a marriage, a shell of a husband, a facade of a family. One night she started to say in front of the children that he wasn't a real husband. That she was married to him, but he wasn't married to her. He became very upset, and phoned the doctor the next morning. This is the sort of statement for which people are sent to see psychiatrists and into hospitals, if they persist.

Jill's mother had a severe stroke in 1963. She recovered to live on, nursed by Jill, until she died two years later. Jill always said that her mother had died in 1963. She did not recognize the woman she nursed for two years as her mother. That was another person. And when her mother "officially" died in 1965, she felt only relief not grief.

The official dates of public events can be out of phase with the structure of experience. If we deny the official definitions of public events, we are regarded as mad. A woman who says, as though she really means it, such things as her mother is dead, when she is alive, and that her husband is not her husband, will soon be regarded as psychotic. Let us call the experiential structure A, and public event B. It sometimes happens that the product of A and B, in a marriage ceremony, is a Marriage. Both people are married in all senses at once. How often that happens I do not know, but I think not often.

I suspect that one of the functions of rituals is to pin A onto B, at certain critical moments in the life of a social group, for example, births, marriages, deaths. In our society many of the old rituals seem to be losing much of their power. And new ones have not arisen.

A and B may seem to float, unattached to each other. In many families they can seem so divorced from each other, it is difficult to see what laws govern their relationship. In order to preserve the convention of sanity, there is a general collusion to disavow A. If anyone breaks this general rule he or she is liable to be invalidated.

Nevertheless, A, avowedly or not, is always being mapped onto B. It is fortunate if our mapping of a particular *range* of public events from the domain of our experience, is not too incongruent. One is not supposed to feel married, if one has not been married. That is cheating. Conversely, one is supposed to feel married, if one "is". If one goes through a marriage by our socially shared conventions, and *experiences* oneself as being married, well and good. If one does not really feel it is "real", if somehow or other it did not seem to "take", if one feels no different, then there are relatives and friends to tell us: "Don't worry, I felt the same, my dear. Wait a little, wait until you have a child. . . . Then you will feel you are a mother," and so on. But if one experiences the marriage ceremony as an *execution*, this is more serious. One is making the mistake, even the *sin*, of mapping A to B, in a way one is definitely not supposed to. One may not be able to help it. But that is how it is felt. So one feels, perhaps, frightened, or guilty, and probably wishes to disavow A completely; to take refuge in B, where everything is just as everyone says it is.

The set of elements that comprise the structure of events as experienced, must then not only be privately *disavowed*, but must be *excommunicated* from the family dialogue. Disavowed, and excommunicated, it does not cease to exist; sometimes it erupts, inrupts, disrupting the cosy chat that has taken the place of genuine dialogue. Genuine dialogues cannot occur without disclosing ourselves to each other, and without according the other, and finding from the other, recognition and acceptance of how we experience one another.

Conventions are necessary. We can't go around saying that people are dead when everyone can see they are alive, or alive when they have been buried, or that the world is crumbling when there it is, as everyone can see, there as usual. At least we can't make such statements without qualifying what we say. But if all A that does not fit B is already disqualified, then we have to make enormous efforts to tailor A to shape and size if we are to avoid serious trouble.

Not all of us are equally gifted in this art. Later I shall allude to some of the *operations* we do on our experience to legitimize it, to make it conform to our "laws" that are often unwritten, often unspoken, often unavowed. This is a matter of the politics of the family.

If this system breaks down, a psychiatrist is liable to be called in – a strategy developed in Europe and North America recently, in the last 150 years.

Let me read you the full account of his intervention into a family by a Professor Morel, a French psychiatrist.

It appeared in his textbook of psychiatry, published in 1860. It is of historical interest because here the term dementia praecox was first introduced. This term is still occasionally used, but it has been generally superseded by the term schizophrenia, together with changes in the concept.

To Morel, dementia praecox was a particularly insidious, inherited, constitutional disease that comes over some young people leading on to a dementia. Morel introduced the term in a passage in his text where he is writing about inherited taints and degeneracies of different kinds. This is his account:[1]

. . . I recall with sorrow a disorder of heredity of a progressive form which appeared in a family with whose members I grew up in my youth. An unhappy father consulted me one day on the mental state of his son, aged 13 to 14, in whom a violent hatred for the author of his being had suddenly replaced the most tender sentiments. When I first saw the child, whose head was well formed and whose intellectual faculties surpassed those of many of his schoolfellows, I was struck by the fact that his growth had been arrested in some way. His chief miseries were related to this apparently futile source, which had nothing to do with peculiar anomalies of his feelings. He was in despair because he was the smallest in his class, although he always came first in 'composition' without any effort and almost without working. It was, so to speak, by intuition that he understood things and that everything classified itself in his memory and intellect. Gradually he lost his gaiety, became sombre, taciturn, and showed a tendency to solitariness. One would have thought that he had onanistic tendencies, but it was not so. The child's statement of melancholy depression and his hatred of his father, which was carried to the length of thinking of killing him, had a different cause. His mother was deranged, alienated, and his grandmother eccentric in the extreme.

I ordered that this child's studies be interrupted and he be isolated in an hydrotherapeutic institution. Gymnastic exercises, baths, manual work, were to enter into the new health-conditions of his existence. These methods were pursued consistently and intelligently by a doctor as knowledgeable as he was enlightened, (Dr. Gillebert d'Hercourt), and a most happy modification was achieved in the organic state of the child. He grew considerably but the situation came to be dominated by another phenomenon just as worrying as those I have already spoken of. The young invalid progressively forgot all that he had learned; his brilliant intellectual faculties underwent a most worrying period of arrest. A kind of torpor akin to stupefaction replaced his former activity, and when I saw him again I judged that the fatal transition

[1]Morel. *Traité des maladies mentales*, 1860, p. 565.

4

to that state of dementia praecox was in course of operation. This despairing prognosis is generally far from the minds of the parents, and even of the doctors who attend these children.

This, nevertheless, is in many cases the mournful end of hereditary madness. A sudden paralysis of all the faculties, a dementia praecox, indicate that the young subject has reached the end of the intellectual life he can expect.

This concise and elegant clinical description is one of the prototypes to have set the scene for what must be well over a million comparable diagnoses under comparable circumstances, in the last 100 years.

With inessential changes in the idiom, the *structure* of this presentation is still the *paradigm* of what happens when most clinical psychiatrists are called in to examine, diagnose and treat a "case".

The presenting complaint is made by an "unhappy father", of a family that Morel knew well. The complaint given is that the son (aged 13 or 14) had "suddenly" evidenced to the father "a violent hatred" of him; whereas, before, his father had been under the impression that his son had "the most tender sentiments" towards him. Morel's first comment on the situation is exclusively about the boy, not even about the whole boy: his head was well formed and intellectually he was above average. However, he was smaller than average. Somehow, such is the spell Morel casts, we already regard this information as beginning to confirm some diagnosis that the great clinician will lead us towards step by step, as a detective leads us to the criminal by a process of exclusion. Clearly there is nothing the matter with the father. That goes without saying. If the boy, according to the father, hates him, there *must* be something the matter with the boy. His head *looks* alright, and he is doing well at school. But he is rather short. Aha! . . . an arrest of development of an inherited constitutional nature. His chief source of misery appears to be that he is small. Aha! This has nothing to do with what is *really* the matter with him, namely, the fact that he hates his father. He has lost his gaiety, he has become sombre, taciturn, and shows a tendency to solitariness: a picture is beginning to take shape. Indeed, a new psychiatric syndrome is about to be invented. Sudden onset; the affects attacked first; evidence of a constitutional arrest of development; . . . must be inherited. To clinch it, it does not appear to be caused by onanism (masturbation). And his mother and his grandmother showed signs of mental disorder. There is no question about it. He needs *treatment*. Immediately.

One hopes for the best, though one fears the worst. We must take him from school and isolate him in an "hydrotherapeutic institution". This will surely stop him hating his father. He grows **a** bit more. But unfortunately, he does not "respond" in other ways. Still, we can tell his father that we did all that could be done to get his son to love him. He has lost all interest in his studies, and will not speak to anyone now. But, look at his mother and grandmother. In those cases, when it is inherited, we are fighting a losing battle. We have to tell you that the chances of recovery are small.

This story is still all too common. Instead of dementia praecox, read process schizophrenia. Instead of "hydrotherapeutic institution", read one of our best hospitals or sanatoria. Instead of "gymnastic exercises, etc.", read group therapy, occupational therapy, milieu therapy. Add a touch of psychotherapy, a sprinkling of electro-shocks for the depression, a dab of hormones for the arrest in his development, and some vitamins and drugs, so as not to deprive him of the benefit of any chance that recent advances in psychiatry can offer. . . .

Why does he hate his father and why had he even thought of killing him? We shall never know, but we can imagine that perhaps, as he grew up, he began to think that maybe his father had driven his mother crazy, and (so we may imagine) his mother had a point when she said (so we are imagining) that his father had one face for the world and another for his family. Maybe.

The essential point is that the direct effect, and intention, of psychiatric intervention is to turn this young man into a "young invalid": to *invalidate* his hatred of his father, under the name of treatment. In a minority of cases, 100 years ago, this treatment worked. Such young persons would decide *not* to hate their father, that is, not to exhibit the "signs" of the "illness" for which they were receiving such "treatment". A few might even learn to be grateful. The main difference is that psychiatry is today more *effective*. In a greater percentage of cases, remission of symptoms can be claimed and the relapse rate is lower. And then a few "maintenance" electro-shocks may suffice, especially if the patient keeps taking his tranquillizers, for some years, until he gets over it.

This boy's father was known to Morel as a good man, and his son, a good boy, who did not masturbate, seems to have hated him. How can the discrepancy between the public image of the father, and the experience to which the boy testifies, be resolved? Certainly not, for Morel, by trying to explore the family structure in which the boy's feelings, I would guess, would find their perfectly intelligible context. Instead, the first thing to do is to examine his head or his psyche. People have been examining the heads, blood and urine or the *psycho*-pathology of such boys and girls ever since.

It does not essentially matter to my present argument whether one is inclined to examine heads, blood, urine, or favours, on the other hand, some pathology exclusively "in" the "psyche". The hunt for the "pathology" and the aetiology of the "disease" goes on just as much by those who are concerned with the psychopathology as with physical pathology. The boy did not hate his father because he was ill: he was turned into an invalid because his hatred for his father was invalidated.

If our wishes, feelings, desires, hopes, fears, perception, imagination, dreams . . . do not correspond to the law, they are outlawed, and excommunicated. Outlawed and excommunicated, they do not cease to exist. But they do undergo secondary transformations.

If A and B are incongruent there is a law against admitting A to the dialogue. If one person blows the gaff, the mind police (psychiatrists) are called in. A crime (illness) is diagnosed. An arrest is made and the patient taken into custody (hospitalization). Interviews and investigations follow.

A confession may be obtained (patient admits he is ill, displays insight). He is convicted either way. The sentence is passed (therapy is recommended). He serves his time, comes out, and obeys the law in future. Some people are refractory to such methods, and their prognosis is therefore regarded as poor. The psychiatrist, who after all is a specialist in these matters, can see one of those refractory cases coming.

In the last paragraph, I have given an account of the official story of psychiatric consultation, examination, diagnosis, prognosis, treatment, in terms of how it is often *experienced* by the patient, namely, as a police operation, etc. If the patient refuses to accept the public definition of this situation, this shows how ill he is. He is paranoid. He is under the delusion that he is being persecuted, by our attempt to help him to realize that he is *not* being persecuted.

Psychiatrists are themselves divided. Some psychiatrists, especially those who have studied families most intensively, have come to the view that much psychiatric practice has been a naive collusion with definition B, and that the matter is much more complex.[2]

Psychiatry is concerned with politics, with who makes the law. Who defines the situation. What is in fact the situation. What is in fact the case, and what is not the case. That is, with ontology.

---

[2]See:

(1) *Intensive Family Therapy.* Edited by Ivan Boszormenyi-Nagy and James L. Framo. Hoeber Medical Division, Harper & Row, New York, 1965.

(2) *Schizophrenia and the Family.* Theodore Lidz, Stephen Fleck, and Alice R. Cornelison. Internat'l. Universities Press, Inc., New York, 1965.

(3) *The Psycho-social Interior of the Family*: A source book for the study of whole families. Ed. Gerald Handel Allen and Unwin Ltd., London, 1968.

(4) *Psychiatry and Anti-Psychiatry.* David Cooper. Tavistock Publications, London, 1967.

Last week I was talking about what people think, feel, experience, is going on, and the public official common-sense definitions of what is happening: and our tendency to invalidate the former when they do not match.

However, the most common situation I encounter in families is when what *I* think is going on bears almost no resemblance to what anyone in the family experiences or thinks is happening, whether or not this coincides with common sense.

Maybe no one knows what is happening. However, one thing is often clear to an outsider: there is concerted family *resistance* to discovering what is going on, and there are complicated stratagems to keep everyone in the dark, and in the dark that they are in the dark.

The truth has to be expended to sustain a family image. The family as a shared fantasy image is usually a container of some kind *in* which all members of the family feel themselves to be, and *for* which image all members of the family may feel each should sacrifice themselves. Since this fantasy exists only in so far as it is "in" everyone who shares "in" it, anyone who gives it up, shatters the "family" in everyone else.[1]

This implies that there is a truth left to expend. When one is a child one is usually taught to believe *by* one's teachers that what one is taught by them is true. We are taught to think we are wrong if we can't see they are right. If one does not believe what they say, there is something wrong with oneself, morally or medi-

[1]Laing, R. D. "Individual and Family Structure." In Lomas, P. (Ed.), *The Predicament of the Family*. Hogarth Press, London, 1967.

cally. One tries to narrow the credibility gap, between what one cannot but help see is going on, and the story that is told, by invalidating one's own senses. What a relief to come across, say, Nietzsche! "The truth is the lie that enables a species to survive." Not because it is necessarily true, but because he was at least able to *think* and say it before he was taken off to the madhouse.

Still, old beliefs die hard. For a long time I clung onto the view, without realizing I was clinging to it, that communication has to do (putting it very crudely) with conveying the truth. This may be true of a railway timetable, and so on. But why should we *assume* this to be the case generally?[2]

Lying is against the rules: children are not supposed to lie to their parents, and they are supposed to believe their parents if or when their parents lie to them. Yet parents may feel guilty to tell the truth, are often embarrassed by it, and may even come to believe their own lies. This can become diabolical.

We would know much more of what is going on if we were not forbidden to do so, and forbidden to realize that we are forbidden to do so. Consequently we may be unblissfully ignorant, in a state ignorant of our ignorance.

Between the truth that is called a lie, and the lie that is called the truth, lies the field of mystification,[3] confusion confounded into false clarity, where images and ideas we imagine and think are real, and that we must preserve, paralyse our imagination and our thinking.

It seems to be done, in part, by a kind of projection. Each generation projects onto the next, elements derived from a product of at least three factors.

What was

    (1) *projected* onto it by prior generations,

    (2) *induced* in it by prior generations, and

    (3) its response to this projection and induction.

If I project an element x from set A onto an element y of set

[2]According to one linguist: "voluntary communication can scarcely have been called upon except to deceive; language must have been invented for the purpose of lying". (*An Introduction to Linguistic Science*. E. H. Sturtevant, Yale University Press Inc., 1960, p. 49.)

[3]Laing, R. D. "Mystification, Confusion and Conflict", Ch. 9 in *Intensive Family Therapy*. Ed by Ivan Boszormenyi-Nagy and James L. Framo. Hoeber Medical Division, Harper & Row, New York, 1965.

B, and if we call the operation of projection or mapping ϕ, then y is the image of x under ϕ.

As we say, Johnny is the "image" of his grandfather. This is not a simple matter.

There is always a projection or a mapping of one *set* of relations onto another *set* of relations. These are relations in time as well as space. In this type of projection or mapping, the *temporal* sequence may be retained or altered.

Projection (as other operations we shall consider later) is usually unknown to the people who are involved. Different mappings are usually going on, simultaneously.

Pure projection is not enough. Having become images of ghostly relations under the operation of projection, we have to be *induced* to *embody* them in our own lives: to enact, unbeknown to ourselves, a shadow play, as images, of images of images . . . of the dead, who have in their turn embodied and enacted such dramas projected upon them, and induced in them, by those before them.

A simple way to get someone to *do* what one wants, is to give an order. To get someone to *be* what one wants him to be, or supposes he is or is afraid he is (whether or not this is what one wants), that is, to get him to embody one's projections, is another matter. The best way is, within a hypnotic (or similar) context, not to tell him what *to* be, but to tell him what he is. Such *attributions,* in context, are many times more powerful than orders (or other forms of coercion or persuasion). An instruction to the other may not be defined as an instruction. It is my impression that we receive most of our earliest and most lasting instructions in the form of attributions. We are told that such and such is the case. One is, say, told that one *is* a good or a bad boy or girl, not only instructed *to be* a good or bad boy or girl. One may be subject to both, but if one *is* (this or that), it is not necessary to be told to be what one has already been "given to understand" one is. The essential medium for communication of this kind is probably not verbal language. Such attributions have the function of instructions or injunctions. This function is or may be denied, giving rise to one type of *mystification*, akin to, or identical with, hypnotic suggestion. My hunch is that what is usually called hypnosis is an experimental model, of a naturally occurring phenomenon in many families. In the family situation, however, the hypnotists (the parents) are already hypnotized (by their parents) and are carrying out their instructions, by bringing their children up to bring their children up . . . in such a way, that includes not realizing that one is carrying out instructions: since one instruction is not to think that one is thus instructed. This is a state easily induced under hypnosis.

One may tell someone to feel something and not to remember that he has been told. It is better simply to tell him *that* he feels it. Better still, tell a third party, in front of him, that he feels it.

Under hypnosis, he feels it; and does not know that he has been hypnotized to feel it. How much of what we ordinarily feel, is what we have all been hypnotized to feel? How much of who we are, is what we have been hypnotized to be?

Your word is my command. A relationship of one to another may be of such power that you become what I take you to be, at my glance, at my touch, at my cough. I do not need to say anything. An attribution, as I am using the term, may be kinetic, tactile, olfactory, visual. Such an attribution is equivalent to an instruction to be obeyed "implicitly".

So, if I hypnotize you, I do not say: I order you to feel cold. I indicate to you that it is cold. You immediately *feel* cold. I think many children begin *in* a state like this.

We indicate to them how it is: they take up their positions in the space we define. They may then choose to become a fragment of that fragment of their possibilities, we indicate they are.

What we explicitly *tell* them to be, is of much less account.

What we indicate they are, is, in effect, an instruction for drama: a scenario.

For example, a naughty child is a role in a particular family drama. We shall see that such a drama is a continuous production. His parents tell him he *is* naughty, because he does not do what they tell him. What they tell him he *is*, is *induction,* far more potent than what they tell him to do. Thus through the attribution: "You are naughty", they are effectively telling him *not to do* what they are ostensibly telling him to do. We are likely to find that such words as: "You are naughty", are the least of it. One is likely to find that the child is being induced to behave as he is by tactile-kinetic-olfactory-visual signals: and that this is part of a whole "secret" communications network, dissociated from the official verbal communiqués.

These signals do not tell him to be naughty; they define what he does *as* naughty. In this way, he learns that he *is* naughty, and how to be naughty in his particular family: it is a learned skill. Some children have a special aptitude for it.

I do not mean that this is the only way a child becomes naughty, but it is one way.

Thus:

Not: Do what I tell you *to* do

But: You will do what I indicate you *are* doing

You will see what I show you, you see

Not: Be what I tell you to be

But: You will be what I indicate you are.

The clinical hypnotist *knows* what he is doing; the family hypnotist almost never. A few parents have described this technique to me as a deliberate stratagem.

More often parents are themselves confused by a child who does *x*, when they tell him to *do y* and indicate he is *x*.

"I'm always trying to get him to make more friends, but he is so self-conscious. Isn't that right, dear?"

"He's so naughty. He never does what I tell him. Do you?"

"I keep telling him to be more careful, but he's so careless, aren't you?"

When such indications or attributions,[4] and instructions are dis-

[4] All the media of communication may carry these quasi-hypnotic indicators (attributions). The way things are said (paralinguistics) rather than the "content" (linguistics). The movements we use (kinesics and parakinesics). And touch, taste, smell. The most intensive systematic study of kinesics has been conducted for some years by Professor Birdwhistell of Eastern Pennsylvanian Psychiatric Institute, and his associates. No systematic data, as far as I know, has been gathered on taste and smell. At the University of Florida Professor Jourard (1) has made a beginning of a study of our touching habits, but so far has not carried his studies into families. Dr. Harry Wiener (2) of New York Medical College, has published a series of highly suggestive speculations on the way our social conduct may be partially controlled by external chemical messengers (ECM) or *ecto* hormones, as we know the intricate social co-ordination of some insects to be, opening up a vast and hitherto almost entirely unexplored field of human studies: the relation of ecto hormones to social behaviour in man.

(1) Sidney M. Jourard. *Disclosing Man to Himself.* Van Nostrand Co. Inc., 1968.

(2) Harry Wiener. "External Chemical Messengers," Parts I to V in New York State Journal of Medicine, Vols. 66, 67, 68 (1966, 67, 68).

discrepant, the two systems of family politics are more evident.

But if there is no discrepancy, if there is a smooth "normal" state of affairs, the structure is less evident, but not essentially different. It is more disguised, masked, and the task of resolving a discrepancy which is not supposed to exist does not have to be undertaken, at this particular juncture. Moreover, if it all seems to work, no one is likely to want to see how it works:

"He knows right from wrong himself: I've never had to tell him not to do these things."

"He does it without me having to ask him."

"He knows himself when he has had enough."

The smoothly working family system is much more difficult to study than one that is in difficulties.

· · ·

There are usually great resistances against the process of mapping the past onto the future coming to light, in any circumstances. If anyone in a family begins to realize he is a shadow of a puppet, he will be wise to exercise the greatest precautions as to whom he imparts this information.

It is not "normal" to realize such things. There are a number of psychiatric names, and a variety of treatments, for such realizations.

I consider that the majority of adults (including myself) are or have been, more or less, in a post-hypnotic trance, induced in early infancy: we remain in this state until – when we dead awaken, as Ibsen makes one of his characters say, we shall find that we have never lived.

Any attempt to wake up before our time is heavily punished, especially by those who love us most. Because, they, bless them, are asleep. They think anyone who wakes up, or, who still asleep, realizes that what is taken to be real is a "dream", is going crazy. Anyone in this transitional state is likely to be confused. To indicate that this confusion is a sign of illness, rather than the possibly confused beginning of true sanity, is the quickest and surest way to create psychosis. The person who realizes that "this is all a nightmare", is afraid he is going crazy. A psychiatrist who professes to be a healer of souls, but who in fact keeps people asleep, treats them for waking up, and helps them to go to sleep again (increasingly effectively as this field of technology sharpens its weapons), will both help to drive him really crazy, *and* confirm the patient's worst fears.

The most awake people I have met, are most aware of this. They are few. They are not necessarily psychotic, nor well-known intellectuals. A celebrated philosopher told me he reckons that he did not awake from this post-infancy hypnotic state till over 50, when he had already written most of the works for which he will long be famous, and in which, among other things, he writes of what I have just been talking.

Freud's *The Interpretation of Dreams* is in part an autobiographical account, of his struggle to wake from that enveloping state of sleep, within which we sleep the sleep within which we dream our dreams, whose main function, in Freud's view, is to preserve sleep, but which can also be the royal road to the unconscious: that is to say, to becoming conscious. *Wo es was, soll ich werden.*

Here are two comparatively simple examples of different types of projection or mapping. Consider not only the projection (as is usually done) from the point of view of the psychology of the projec*tor*: but reflect also on the possible effects on the person projec*ted* upon. What may such projections help to *induce* in the projected-upon? This question runs through all these talks. No one has the answer, but we are the answer.

Freud[5] gives this account of a vision that was described to him by a woman of 40:

One morning she opened her eyes and saw her brother in the room, though, as she knew, he was in fact in an insane asylum. Her small son was sleeping in the bed beside her. To save the child from having a *fright* and *falling into convulsions* when he saw his uncle, she pulled the sheet over his face, whereupon the apparition vanished. This vision was a modified version of a memory from the lady's childhood; and, though it was conscious, it was intimately related to all the unconscious material in her mind. Her nurse had told her that her mother (who had died very young, when my patient was only eighteen months old) had suffered from epileptic or hysterical *convulsions,* which went back to a *fright* caused by her brother (my patient's uncle) appearing to her

[5]Freud, S. Standard Edition. Hogarth Press, London, Vol. V, 1958, p. 545.

disguised as a ghost with a sheet over his head. Thus the vision contained the same elements as the memory: the brother's appearance, the sheet, the fright and its results. But the elements had been arranged in a different context and transferred on to other figures. [Freud's italics.]

On the most superficial level, there would seem to be two sets of relations:

Set A
    her nurse
    her mother
    and her uncle, her mother's brother
and Set B
    the woman herself
    her son
    and her brother, her son's uncle

Under the operation of ϕ (see page 11) her brother appears to her in relation to her son, as (according to her nurse, according to . . . ?) her mother's brother (disguised as a ghost) had appeared to her mother.

She protects her son (ϕ mother) from her brother (ϕ uncle)

Set A	ϕ	*Set B*
Mother	$\longrightarrow$	son
Her mother's brother	$\longrightarrow$	her brother
(her uncle)		(her son's uncle)

Note that "her" "mother", is the image of her nurse's image of her mother.

Consider what ϕ-value we may infer *she* may have assumed in view of the transformations already reported. Freud comments: "The obvious motive of the vision, *or of the thoughts which it replaced* [my italics] was her concern lest her little boy might follow in the footsteps of his uncle, whom he greatly resembled physically."

Freud is proposing that the woman already "sees" her brother "in" her son, is frightened that her son will take after his uncle who is mad, so she overlays this projection with another, namely, of her mother as refracted to her through her nurse.

Freud sees immediately that his patient sees her brother in her son. She is frightened her son will take after his uncle.

A little boy puts a sheet over his head to disguise himself as a ghost and scare his sister. She does not "get over" her fright, but gets married, has a son and a daughter, and dies. When her daughter grows up and has a son, she sees her brother (now actually in a mental hospital) appear in the room where her son is sleeping; in order to protect her son, she puts the sheet over *his* head.

In her best efforts to avoid the dreadful from happening, Freud's patient is bringing it about, by placing the mantle of the ghost over the head of her sleeping son.

A play with shadows. The sheet over the head of a little boy frightening his sister, is pulled over the head of his sister's daughter's son, by a niece whom he may never have met. A ghost in a story told by a nurse to a little girl about when her mother was little, haunts the life of a little boy who has yet to discover his nightmare. The sheet covers the eyes of the little boy, from a vision he has not yet learned to see.

Freud's patient's vision renders visible to us a tiny fragment of the veil of maya which is no other than a projection by ourselves, from ourselves, on ourselves, of ourselves. *We* ourselves are the veil.

Here is the second example.

Mrs. Clark, a harassed mother of four children (three boys and a girl) tells me that she can't do anything with her third son, a teenager called David. He stays out till all hours, he won't tell her what he is up to when he is out, will hardly speak to her when he is in. She can't get to the bottom of him, and he doesn't seem the least concerned that she is so concerned.

Her husband was one of two brothers. His father is dead; his mother is alive. His brother married first and had two sons. He married and his mother, after two sons and two grandsons, very much wanted a granddaughter. But they had a son. Her husband was very pleased and called him after his father. This son is the spitting image of him, as he is of *his* father. The second son was not a girl, and they agreed to try again to try to give Grannie the present of a granddaughter. But they had David who was called after his mother's father who had died shortly before he was conceived. Then they thought they would try once more, and this time, Grannie got her present.

Who does David take after? According to Mrs. Clark and *her* mother, he is just like what Mrs. Clark was like when she was his age. And who did she take after when she was a teenager? According to Mrs. Clark and her mother, she took after her father: as her mother goes on to say, he used to stay out till all hours. He wouldn't tell her what he was up to, he would hardly speak to her when he was at home. She could never get to the bottom of him, and he didn't seem the least concerned that she was so upset.

It seems that Mrs. Clark's father had a daughter who "took after" him for a while, and eventually produced *her* father in *his* grandson, David. If David is already his own grandfather, we might expect him to marry his grandmother, produce his mother in his daughter who will marry his father and produce him, or rather his grandfather, once more in the person of his grandson, who will. . . . But who was his grandfather?

There is a rather complex play going on between David, his mother and grandmother, and between them and the dead grandfather.

The projection of a few attributions formerly made about grandfather onto the grandson, is only one component of a much larger operation, perpetuating itself across many generations. We can perhaps just begin to glimpse its dramatic structure.

History continues to repeat itself, with variations. A teenage grandson cannot play quite the same part as a 70-year-old grandfather. He certainly did not see his "dropping out" as part of a scenario constructed long before he was born, even though his girl friend dresses up in the very latest fashions from London's Portobello Road, in the clothes of his grandfather's *mother*. But it would still be naive to assume that his grandfather may finally get the woman he always wanted. Who was his mother?

Through these labyrinthine paths, the dream or nightmare of one generation comes to be enacted generations later, too late to be true.

The convulsions of a dead grandmother at the ghostly apparition of her brother, are intertwined round the life of a little boy whose mother fears that he will take after her brother.

A mother and daughter continue the play, finding in the grandson a replacement for the grandfather.

The play goes on. The actors come and go. A death leaves a vacancy, to be filled sometimes by one yet to be conceived, or who *has* to be conceived to keep the cast up to strength. Who can better replace a grandfather, than a grandson?

The new member of the cast is induced to embody a part in the ongoing drama. It is not precise, or enough, to say: David is identified with his grandfather. I would rather say: David is given a part comparable to the part his grandfather played. The players should be distinguished from the parts they play, even though the two are often confused by the players themselves.

It is often not difficult to construct an approximate scenario for a two- or three-generational scrap of such plays.

Daughter sides with her easy-going, relatively absent father against nagging mother; without adequate support from him, succumbs to mother. Both rediscover loved and hated husband-father in grandson-son . . . and so on.

A scenario is a set of instructions for a play. But these scenarios, if they exist, are unwritten, and, if a part of a scenario sometimes appears in the lines of the play itself, those who enunciate it are usually deeply unaware that they are doing so.

In my own early life, I was often told that I was going to take after my grandfather; not immediately, but *when I grew up*. We are given such indications as we come out of the womb, on how to go into our graves. They may be implanted before one is five years of age, with instructions not to begin to act them out until 50 years later.

The foregoing examples were among the simplest I could find, and both are further simplified in recounting.

Almost all of us live almost all of our lives in families. First our family of origin; then, when we marry and have children, our so-called nuclear family, the family of origin for our children.

Through this chain of family systems, the fundamental rules that determine our culture are transmitted. We know practically nothing about it.

As the proverbial Irishman said when shown the excessively intricate machine, all parts working away. Yes, I see it works in practice but does it work in theory?

•   •   •

Two intrinsic difficulties face us in studying families. First, the time scale. Families (of some kind or other, albeit *very* different from ours) have existed, say, for at least 100,000 years. We can study directly only a minute slice of the family chain: three generations, if we are lucky. Even studies of three generations are rare. What patterns can we hope to find, when we are restricted to three out of at least 4,000 generations?

A second difficulty is that the more smoothly they function, the more difficult to study.

We can take a watch to pieces and put it together again. We can invent one: learn to make one. We can find out things about it by interfering with it. And so on. Very few of the ways natural scientists have of studying the systems they study, are open to us in studying families, especially those aspects of families that I am discussing with you.

We cannot expect to catch the curtain going up or down in a drama we are born into. But there are plays within plays within plays.

Take any piece of paper. Draw anything on it. Crumple it up. It is not all that easy to express precisely in what way the flat and crumpled patterns are similar and differ.

The more one studies families in detail, the more it becomes apparent that patterns are spread over generations. They undergo transformations. No one, as far as I know, has found out whether these patterns and their transformations *can* be expressed in terms that at present we call mathematical. This is understandable. We ourselves, all of us, are ourselves the elements of the pattern that we are trying to discern. Family patterns are not laid out before us like the stars in the sky.

Notes endowed with such awareness that they are only just able to glimpse the existence of the chord whose elements they are. Perhaps, from the interpenetration of their vibrations they may even begin to infer something in and beyond them, that requires both their life and their death. We call it music: that disdains to be heard by the notes that comprise it.

We are acting parts in a play, that we have never read and never seen, whose plot we don't know, whose existence we can glimpse, but whose ending I do not dare to presume to imagine.

The world, as Hegel puts it, is "a unity of the given and the constructed". It is difficult to determine what is "given" and what are our "constructions". One way is to compare the ways people in different times and places, and even in the same time and place, experience the world. All of us have been, or will be, surprised, even incredulous, when we come across the data of anthropology for the first time, at how vast are the differences between ways of experiencing.

We know very little in detail about how this comes about. We can say for certain that children are not born experiencing the world as we do, as adults, in a particular culture.

They construe the original "given" in ways we as adults once have done, but have forgotten. The study of early childhood experience is a very difficult subject: since children cannot tell us, in our language, how they are experiencing, and we cannot remember.

Our adult experience is a very sophisticated product of many procedures.

The laws governing our experience, I presume, are both natural and social. At a certain level of realization, it is important to distinguish between natural and social laws.

"The Mesopotamian Universe – because it did not consist of dead matter, because every stone, every tree, every conceivable thing in it was a being with a will and character of its own – was . . . founded on authority; its members, too, willingly and automatically obeyed orders which made them act as they should act. These orders we call the laws of nature."[1]

[1]Professor Thorkild Jacobsen: quoted by S. H. Hooke in *Babylonian and Assyrian Religion*. Blackwell, Oxford, 1962, p. 78.

The "deeper" social laws are implanted in us, the more "hard-programmed", the more "pickled" into us, the more like "natural" laws they come to appear to us to be. Indeed, if someone breaks such a "deeply" implanted social law, we are inclined to say that he is "unnatural".

I want to allude to some of the most seemingly "natural" features of contemporary experience, acquired in families, when we are very young.

We construe the given in terms of *distinctions,* according to *rules.* We perform *operations* on our experience, in order to comply with the rules. By these operations, according to the rules, in terms of the distinctions, a normal product is generated, if all goes according to plan.

We make distinctions, but we are not born with the distinctions we make ready made.

I suppose that there is a set of primitive distinctions in terms of which we construe what presents itself: and that our first experience is the first product of our most primitive constructions and the *virgin* given. This product subsequently *appears* to be given. Compared to our adult experience, this "original" experience is "virginal" or innocent. But *any* experience wherein the given is distinguished in any way, is not innocent and not given, though it may seem to be. We are free to apply our terms in different ways, but our set of terms is as determined for us as the phonemes (sound units) of our language.

I suppose that distinctions are acquired, and acquired very early.

A set of primitive distinctions are formed.

Rules govern the formation of this set and the operations that are performed on this set.

My guess is that by one year from birth, the following distinctions, among others, have come to be made: distinctions between

1. inside and outside
2. pleasure and pain, pleasant-unpleasant
3. real and not-real
4. good and bad
5. me and not-me
6. here and there
7. then and now.

For present purposes it does not matter at what age these distinctions have been made: or even what the distinctions are. My essential point is that *some* distinctions come to be *made*, somehow or other, some time or other: that these distinctions did not exist in the first place. With these distinctions, we work upon the *prima materia*, of the given. Our experience is a product, formed according to a recipe, a set of rules for what distinctions to make, when, where, on what. Rules are themselves distinctions in action. Operations between distinctions already constructed are carried out continually according to further rules.

Thus: I slice my experience into inside-outside: into real-unreal: into good and bad: into me and not me: into here and there: into now and then; I find it pleasant or painful.

Let us suppose: inside-me-here-now-good-real-pleasant applies to the same slice. Then, you may feel I am a lucky man. This does not mean that if all of me is good, all that is real is me: nor that if I am here-now, I was not there-then. But I have achieved a very highly prized identity in our culture. What hell to arrive at: me-unreal-bad-here-inside-now-pain. This is common.

Let us take a brief look at one of our fundamental distinctions – that between inside and outside. It cannot be considered for long in isolation from the other distinctions we make: this distinction (as all others) operates with other distinctions according to syntactical rules for their combination. The inside-and-outside distinction is applied to almost all facets of experience. I can hardly *not* make this distinction. Very seldom will I drop it. Imagine the following actions:

    (i) swallow the saliva in your mouth
   (ii) take a glass of water: sip it and swallow it
  (iii) spit in it, swallow spit and water
  (iv) sip some water: spit it back, sip and swallow what you
        have spat back.

You may be able to do all four, easily, but many people cannot, and are disgusted especially at (iii) and (iv).

One is aware that there is a difference between saliva inside one's mouth, and that same saliva, one inch in space, outside one's mouth.

There is an even sharper differential in terms of faeces, inside or outside.

We feel ourselves to be inside a bag of skin: what is outside this bag, is not-us. Me – inside. Not-me – outside.

In ecstatic moments, this distinction is lost. Making love, starvation, listening to music, high fever. Few people have not experienced its loss, but few have experienced its loss often, or for long (such is my impression).

These moments are privileged exceptions. Under usual circumstances inside/outside is one of the distinctions which, combined together with other distinctions by rules of an experiential syntax, seem to help towards giving us a sense that our experience makes sense. It belongs to the familial-social order, not to the natural order.

Yet the syntax of common sense is as obscure as it is obvious. How difficult things would be if we went about in a modern city, not able to take it for granted that I am inside my skin and outside yours, and you are inside your skin and outside mine!

But difficulties arise. "I" am inside my skin, but I may feel outside what is inside me and outside all I am not inside. Where then am I? Not quite inside anything? Not quite outside anything? What do I want to be inside? What do I want to be outside? What do I want to be inside me? What do I want to be outside me? Do I want to be inside what is inside me? Do I want to be outside what is inside me? Do I feel inside what is outside me? Is what is inside me, what I would like outside me? Is what is outside me, what I would like inside me? Perhaps I can do an exchange. By projection, put what is inside me, outside me. By introjection, put what is outside, inside. I have now turned myself inside-out and outside-in. But, despite this exchange I may still feel outside the inside, and inside the outside. Let us introduce the good/bad distinction. Suppose my insides were bad, and by projection, I have put them outside. My bad insides, now outside, persecute me. Or suppose I want to get outside what *I* am inside. Difficult, without finding that I have what *I* was inside, inside me. A doubtful improvement. If I am full of goodies inside, they may be stolen by those who have no goodies like me. If I put the goodies outside, then I am empty of goodies, and am dependent for my supplies of goodies from the outside. The attempt to find a satisfactory stable combination between good/bad, empty/full, inside/outside, me/not-me, may take up a great deal of energy – so I shall feel exhausted, empty inside *and* outside. Suppose we add, real and unreal, and true and false, to this infernal dance: to be real is to be genuine, and to be unreal is to be false. I must avoid being unreal, but if I am *inside* reality, reality may be outside, and if I am already empty inside, I may find myself in danger of being empty, unreal, false and bad. But I *want* to be full of reality, true and good. Let's do another exchange. Immediately it is Them who are false, empty, unreal and bad.

But it is not everyone who finds a resting place this way. Suppose to be real is to be *inside* the real, but the outside is unreal because I have put the real inside. So try to put the outside inside again, make the inside real, make the real full, and the full genuine. Then I am good because I am full but bad because I am not full of myself, hence unreal. But can we not distribute things a bit more evenly?

Surely there is enough reality to go round? Let us say: inside me is real, and inside *them* is real. It is real outside me and I am inside reality, and reality is inside myself. So where is unreality? Unreality does not exist, and does not *deserve* to exist.

We, our family, and our family's families, our school, our church, our town, our state and our country, our television and cups and saucers and display cabinet, and our Aunt Jessie, are real: and true; we can trust each other: and we have a full life. The world comes to our town; and if we sometimes do wrong: we do our best. We don't wish any evil on anyone. We *are*. And those to whom *we* do not exist, do not exist, and, if we can help it, shall not exist.

Because we must defend *reality* against the emptiness, deceit, and the evil, of *Unreality*. That is what we are fighting for. To defend the real against the unreal, the true against falsehood, the full life against an empty life, the good against evil. What is, against what is not.

But then, what are we defending ourselves against? Nothing? Oh no! The danger, the menace, the enemy, Them, are very real. So we have to start again. . . .

They Are Real. They are dangerous, because they *are*. So long as they *are*, we are in danger. So we must destroy them. If we must destroy them, they must destroy us to prevent us destroying them, and we must destroy them before they destroy us before we destroy them before they destroy us . . . which is where we are at the moment.

They cannot *both* be unreal and non-existent, real and exist, unreal and exist, or real and not exist. *They* exist to be destroyed and are destroyed to be reinvented.

We need not worry that the kill ratio between Them and Us will get too high. There are always more where *they* came from. From *inside Us*.

Given our distinctions and our rules, we have to *work* to normalize our experience. We could never succeed unless we were able to employ a further set of operations on our experience to some of which I have already alluded. Most of these are described in psychoanalysis as "defence mechanisms".

Denial is one of the simplest.

> "This is the case" is changed to: "This is *not* the case"; e.g., "I feel jealous" is changed to: "I do *not* feel jealous."

Splitting. A set is partitioned into two subsets.

> In a complete split, no traffic is allowed to occur between the two subsets.

Displacement.

> e.g., I feel angry at Tom, *instead* of Dick.
>
> I come back and "take it out" on the wife, for what I feel about the Boss.

Scotomatization.

> I do not see what I do not want to.

Replacement.

> I see something else instead.

Projection.

> I map inside onto outside.

Introjection.

> I map outside onto inside.

Rationalization.

> I give myself a cover-story.

Repression.

> Forgetting and forgetting one has forgotten.

Regression.

> Going back.

Identification.

Two separate subsets are taken to be one.

Mystification.

Misdefinition of the issues.

Reversal.

I hate him is reversed to: He hates me.

Many more are described in psychoanalytic literature, including inversion, reaction-formation, isolation, reduplication, turning against the self, undoing, idealization, derealization.

The definitive work remains to be written on this subject. The present list is not well classified, because some of these "defences" are simple, and others made up of two or three simple operations. The subject is a very difficult one in the technical literature; there are overlaps in connotation between terms: different authors do not use the same term in the same way: the literature is in three principal languages: German, English and French, giving rise to problems of translation: Freud's own theorizing, in this and other respects, evolved and changed, through over 40 years.

Operations apply additional constraints on the product. They "cancel" and substitute what is in accord with rules, and they do this according to rules that govern the operations themselves. If experience (E) is permitted to be pleasant or *ought* to be pleasant E will be operated upon to make it more seemingly pleasant. But if the rules do not permit or demand this, if pleasure is forbidden or despised, then "pleasure" will be sacrificed for other values higher on the hierarchy.

Most operations on E are themselves operated upon to render them as we say "unconscious". Only as we manage to neutralize these operations on operations can our operations on E become themselves elements of E, such that we can examine them. Until we can do this, we have to *infer* them. Such an inference as to their existence may itself be blocked by such operations as denial, scotomatization.

The operations on experience we are discussing, are commonly not experienced themselves. So seldom does one ever catch oneself in the act, that I would have been tempted to regard them as themselves, *essentially* not elements of experience, had I not occasionally been able to catch a glimpse of them *in action* myself, and had not others reported the same to me. It is comparatively easy to catch someone else in the act. This leads me to propose that there is an operation, or a class of operations, that *operates on our experience of our operations,* to cancel them from our experience: operations of this latter class somehow operate on our experience of *themselves,* whereby we neither experience our first operations nor the operations that shut the former operations out of our experience. This is particularly clear in the case of repression.

When I was 13, I had a very embarrassing experience. I shall not embarrass you by recounting it. About two minutes after it happened, I caught myself in the process of putting it out of my mind. I had already more than half forgotten it. To be more precise, I was in the process of sealing off the whole operation by forgetting that I had forgotten it. How many times I had done this before I cannot say. It may have been many times because I cannot remember many embarrassing experiences before that one, and I have no (1) memory of (2) such an *act* of forgetting I was forgetting before 13. I am sure this was not the first time I had done that trick, and not the last, but most of these occasions, so I believe, are still so effectively repressed, that I have still forgotten that I have forgotten them.

This is repression. It is not a simple operation. We forget something. And forget that we have forgotten it. So as far as we are subsequently concerned, there is nothing we have forgotten. It is very effective.

A clean-cut operation of repression achieves a *cut-off*, such that

(a) we forget X

(b) we are unaware that there is an X that we have forgotten

(c) we are unaware that we have *forgotten* X

(d) and unaware that we are unaware that we have forgotten we have forgotten X.

Repression is the annihilation, not only *from* the memory of, but *of* the memory of, a part of E, *together with,* the annihilation of the experience of the operation. It is a product of at least three operations.

When we consider any actual instance of any operations, we find that it is almost impossible to find a pure example of a single operation in isolation. This is what we might expect. It does not mean, because a baby moves all the fingers of one hand at once, that it has not five fingers. Denial and displacement form a common operation product. "It's not *my* fault. It's your fault." Denial and displacement can equal projection.

Wish-fulfillment and idealization are varieties of operation entailing projection and denial. All projection involves some measure of denial of the range of E. I am unhappy. I am *not* unhappy (denial). I am *not* denying that I am unhappy (denial of denial).

I take the principal function of all these operations to be: the production and maintenance of E, that is at best desired, at least tolerated, in the family by the family in the first place.

The operations I have alluded to are operations on one's own experience. They are done by one person to himself or herself. But they would be unnecessary unless the rules of the family required them: and ineffectual unless others co-operate. Denial is demanded by the others: it is part of a *transpersonal system of collusion,* whereby we comply with the others, and they comply with us. For instance, one requires collusion to play "Happy Families". Individually, I am unhappy. I deny I am to *myself*; I deny I am denying anything to *myself* and to the others. They must do the same. I must collude with their denial and collusion, and they must collude with mine.

> So we are a happy family and we have no
> secrets from one another.
> *If* we are unhappy/we have to keep it a secret/
> and we are unhappy that we have to keep it a secret
> and unhappy *that* we have to keep secret/the fact/that
>   we *have* to keep it a secret
> and that we *are* keeping all that secret.
> But since we are a happy family you can see
> this difficulty does not arise.

Repression of a great deal of infant sexuality is sanctioned, the act of repression is itself denied, and repression, its sanction and the denial of repression, are denied. Nothing has happened. "I don't know what you're talking about." For instance, who ever heard of a good boy, and a normal man, *ever,* having wanted to suck his father's penis? It is quite normal, at one time, to have wanted to suck his mother's breast. However, it is on the whole best not to connect mother's breast and girl friend's breast, or, if one is a woman, woman's breast with boy friend's genitals. It is safest, on the whole, to keep these sets of relations in separate partitions (splitting), and *repress*, to be even more on the safe side, *all infantile desires* in case they were too "perverse", since they antedate partitioning and repression, etc., *and* to deny the existence of any such operations of partitioning and repression, and to deny this denial. The product arrived at is the outcome of many rules without which it could not be generated or maintained, but to admit the rules would be to admit what the rules and operations are attempting to render non-existent.

One is expected to be capable of passion, once married, but not to have experienced too much passion (let alone acted upon it) too much before. If this is too difficult, one has to pretend first not to feel the passion one really feels, then, to pretend to passion one does *not* really feel, and to pretend that certain passionate upsurges of resentment, hatred, envy, are unreal, or don't happen, or are something else. This requires false realizations, false de-realizations, and a cover-story (rationalization). After this almost complete holocaust of one's experience on the altar of conformity, one is liable to feel somewhat empty, but one can try to fill one's emptiness up with money, consumer goods, position, respect, admiration, envy of one's fellows for one's business, professional, social success. These together with a repertoire of distractions, permitted or compulsory, serve to distract one from one's own distraction: and if one finds oneself overworked, under too great a strain, there are perfectly approved additional lines of defence, concoctions to taste of, narcotics, stimulations, sedatives, tranquilizers to depress one further so that one does not know how depressed one is and to help one to over-eat and over-sleep. And there are lines of defence beyond *that*, to electro-shocks, to the (almost) final solution of simply removing sections of the offending body, especially the central nervous system. This last solution is necessary, however, only if the *normal social* lobotomy does not work, and chemical lobotomy has also failed.

I can think of no way of generating a "normal" product from the stuff of our original selves except in some such way: once we arrive at our matrix of distinctions, we have rules for combining and partitioning them into sets and subsets. The "normal" product requires that these operations are themselves denied. We like the food served up elegantly before us: we do not want to know about the animal factories, the slaughter-houses and what goes on in the kitchen. Our own cities are our own animal factories; families, schools, churches are the slaughter-houses of our children; colleges and other places are the kitchens. As adults in marriages and business, we eat the product.

BEYOND REPRESSION:
RULES AND METARULES

The distinctions and the operations I was describing last week are pervasive. Generally, we are very aware of such distinctions, but not nearly so aware that we *make* them. The operations I described are usually not experienced at all. Yet with their help most of us flesh out a world of sorts. With great labour, a wish is

 (i) denied
 (ii) replaced by a fear that generates a nightmare that is
 (iii) denied, and on which a
 (iv) nice facade is then placed
 (denial, replacement, denial, replacement) – a comparatively simple, four-step sequence.

Almost any operations are sanctioned if they help to serve up a "normal" product. It is *difficult* to behave sufficiently "normally" to get by, without using some such tricks. If one gives them up and still can't get out of the social system that is largely built upon them, is perpetuated by them, and generates and perpetuates them in turn, one may still have to lie on a bed of nails. Difficult to pretend to enjoy it, once one has realized that it is not a bed of roses.

Not only are such operations permitted, they may be *demanded*. Projection and the denial of it is demanded. It is mandatory to project bad onto what is the Enemy whoever they may be: and it is *mandatory* to deny that this is projection.

One can lay out a *projection* map for the whole cosmos shaded or coloured, as to what regions we must or must not project what onto: a map for a map, as it were.

To take the simplest schema. Let us suppose each region is

governed by a rule about good/bad. Suppose values for each region are set as (+) good, or (−) bad, (+ or −) optional, or neutral (neither + nor −).

There is said to be a *time* and place for everything. At home:

(1) one must *not* put mother's pearl necklace down the w.c.

(2) one *must* put something down the w.c. and nowhere else

(3) one must *not* go to bed with one's boots on

(4) one *must* brush one's teeth before going to sleep

(5) one must *not* make bad smells at dinner table

and so on. Such rules are liable to be rather exact, and stringent.

The rules governing what values the whole cosmos is to be endowed with are equally stringent.

There are times and places and people for

(1) + values (good)

(2) − values (bad)

(3) + or − values (optional)

(4) neither + nor − (o) value (neutral)

(the stars must be regarded as neither good nor bad, if one is "normal").

We can add an open fifth category for regions that one may regard as good (+), or bad (−), or optional (+ or −), or neutral (o). They are few. Can you think of any?

If there is perfect coincidence between the value we project and the value allotted to a range, everything is in its proper time and place. There is no infringement of the rules on this set of issues, and no need for guilt or anxiety on these grounds.

When positive values are mapped on a positive range, one thinks well of those one is supposed to think well of. If one is a Christian: God is Good. If one is a Patriot: One's Country is Good. If one is a Black Powerite: the Blacks are Great. One is good one's self if one has good thoughts about what one is supposed to think good about, and bad thoughts about what one is supposed to think bad about. When negative values are mapped onto the positive range, one does not think well of those one is supposed to think well of. When negative values are applied to the negative range, one thinks badly of those one is supposed to think badly about. With positive values to the negative range, one thinks well of those one is supposed to think badly of. With positive or negative values to the optional range, one thinks badly or well of what or of those one is free to take sides over. Neutral values to the neutral range, one does not think well or badly about what one is supposed to think is neither good nor bad. And so on.

Such rules govern the whole social field. Unless we can "see through" the rules, we only see through them. They make social science a peculiarly difficult subject, because the social scientist in one particular society does not simply dissolve the rules because he is a social scientist. "We" can easily see that there is little place for sociology in Russia or China. It is much more difficult for us to see how "our" rules govern the values we map onto the social field. It is difficult even to see that we have values we are mapping let alone see the rules in terms of which such projections are carried out.

In terms of such rules for what values we endow what regions of the world, that is, in terms of our projection map, let us consider evil thoughts.

Evil thoughts are a relationship. It is not what you think, see, feel, intend, imagine, etc., but *what* you think, etc., *about what* or *whom,* when and where.

It is bad to think bad about what you are supposed to think good about. It is bad to think good about what you are supposed to think bad about. It is good to think *bad* about what you're supposed to think *bad* about. It is a bit mad to take seriously what is not supposed to be serious. It is bad to be frivolous about what is supposed to be serious (inappropriate affect). A "good" or a "bad" thought, only becomes Good or Bad in relation to its object: *what* we are thinking about *what.* A bad thought is *good* if applied to a bad object. A good thought is bad if applied to a bad object.

Here are two lists. We can see, that, without any firsthand knowledge whatever of the target person or range, we in our society *know* what attributions we should/should not, apply to whom: father, mother, husband, wife, son, daughter, self: the Whites, the Reds, the Yellows, the Blacks, the Jews, the Goy; good/bad safe/dangerous, trustworthy/untrustworthy, kind/cruel, and so on.

The rules governing our system of projections (attributions), apply to the whole range of the social world system, and indeed of the whole cosmos. Once any part of the social world system comes to be governed by such rules, this means that each part of the social world system

(i) is already endowed with a value by the fact that there is a rule governing it.

(ii) There may be a rule that this value must not be changed, challenged, *questioned*, or even *seen*.

(iii) There may be a rule not only against *seeing* that there *is* such a value, and that there *is* a rule (i), but

(iv) there may be a rule against seeing (ii) and

(v) a rule against seeing (iii) and

(vi) a rule against seeing (iv) and (v) and (vi).

As regards projection, there seem to be rules against seeing that there are such rules, and hence against clearly formulating the problems that arise from complying with them, or of breaking them.

Breaking these rules, and the rules against seeing the rules, and the rules against seeing the rules against seeing the rules, is met by

(1) deterrents in the first place, to forestall any breach of the system, and

(2) punishments in the second place.

But neither deterrence nor punishment can be defined as such in *words*, since such a definition would itself be a breach of the rules against seeing the rules. . . .

The direct breach of basic rules at the first level can be punished by death. The person earns attributions of treason, treachery, heresy: he is liable to be seen as being evil, wicked, depraved, degenerate. People commonly feel that no punishment is good enough for him: he or she ought to be horsewhipped; *and* given the very best treatment: he or she is *bad* and mad (Ezra Pound for example).

Talking about talking about rules about the rules about the rules, as I am doing, is just possible, if I do not push it too far, or be too direct. If I push it further, to be safe, I must become more *abstract*.

Rules govern all aspects of experience, *what* we are to *experience*, and what *not* to experience. And the operations that we must and must not carry out, in order to arrive at a permitted picture of ourselves and others in the world.

Suppose we are told to repair a car engine. And given instructions on *how* to do so, which will inevitably lead to the engine falling apart: and we have instructions *against* operations of putting it together: though we are instructed to feel *bad,* if it is *not* put together.

One may be instructed, if things seem to be going wrong, to examine one's instructions. They may be wrong. They may require adaptation, modification, or to be dropped. But a special situation exists if there is a rule against examining, or questioning rules: and beyond that, if there are rules against even being aware that such rules exist, including this last rule.

If *what* we are instructed to achieve cannot be achieved by the *how* we are instructed to achieve it, we are in difficulties.

We are instructed to be honest. But instructed to operate on our experience in ways that can only be called dishonest.

We are instructed to be trust*ing* of certain others, who tell us that we cannot trust ourselves. So that we are called on to place our untrustworthy trust in those who tell us to trust them when they tell us that we are untrustworthy: hence, our trust is untrustworthy. And so on.

People carry out different operations according to different sets of instructions, to maintain much the same primary distinctions (in our culture) mapped onto the social cosmos, strictly according to the rules. According to what these distinctions are applied to, and how they are applied, different worlds of experience are generated and maintained. If the instructions are contradictory or paradoxical they may lead to distinctions being combined in simultaneous and incompatible sets.

It can happen that it is not even possible to *split* or partition the world into two, three or more bits so that each subset consists of compatible elements.

There are instructions as to *what* we experience. And instructions as to *how* we have to experience what. As with our behaviour. We are told, for instance, to brush our teeth (what to do). And we are told *how* to do so.

Instructions give us more or less responsibility and more or less discretion. For instance: We may be instructed to keep our teeth and gums in good repair. It may be left to our discretion how we do so. If our teeth get rotten, it may or may not be our fault, according to whether we have been instructed to regard this as our responsibility. However, if we are instructed to clean our teeth in a specific way, with a specific sort of toothbrush, and a specific type of toothpaste, to eat certain things that are good for the teeth, and not to eat other things that are bad for the teeth, together with other specific dos and don'ts and if we do the dos and don't do the don'ts – if, that is, we carry out our instructions to the letter – then, *if* our teeth fall out, it is not our fault. But we must search ourselves to find where we have gone wrong, if not in the letter, then in the spirit of the way we carried out our instructions. If things go wrong, so we may have been instructed, it is a punishment. It behoves us to find the crime that fits it. And if we do not find the crime, this failure is a crime. It only serves to show how criminal we are. Our teeth may be falling out, therefore, because although we have eaten only precisely what we should have, and no more than we should, we have *wanted* to eat more or otherwise. Maybe it is a punishment for our greed. Clearly we would be unwise to be wise only *after* the event. So we shall have to go over our instructions "with a fine tooth comb" all the time, in search of any fault that might be punished by our teeth falling out, or worse. But is this constant self-examination not itself a fault: a form of self-indulgence, or narcissism, egotism, pride, self-importance? What else can one do, created frail, commanded to be sound? We must pray. But would we not be wise to have all our teeth removed, both to avoid them falling out, and to mortify our flesh for its self-indulgence and our spirit for its sins against the flesh? For especially if one cannot find what they are, one has been instructed to realize that such failure betokens the greatest depth of sin: to be so sunk in depravity that one cannot even see one's depravity. If one cannot see one's depravity, this failure to see one's depravity is a depravity, more depraved than all other depravities. . . .

No one intended, when they told a little boy when and how to clean his teeth, and that his teeth would fall out if he was bad, together with Presbyterian Sunday School and all the rest of it, to produce 45 years later the picture of a typical obsessive involutional depression. This syndrome is one of the specialities of Scotland.

Two or more instructions may be incompatible. This engenders, at least viewed structurally, a comparatively simple type of conflict. I tell you to do both A and B, but you can't do the one if you do the other. We can become tied in much more complex knots. I can do no more than indicate some aspects of this subject, which is only beginning to be studied by a few people.[1]

If I tell you to do something, this does not explicitly tell you to tell yourself that you are doing it because I told you. I may tell you to do something and be quite prepared to let you tell yourself (if you wish, if it makes you feel any better), that you are doing it because you want to, *not* because you have been told to. On the other hand, *you* may want to do something, but see that I like to feel that you want to do what I tell you, so you get me to tell you to do what you want to do, so that you will be doing what you want, and what you are told at the same time.

However, this may embarrass me, so I order you to (i) do what *I* want (ii) but among the things I want is that you, in doing what *I* want, do not *think* that you are doing what I want, but that you are doing what *you* want, and, even, far from that being what I want, it is what I *don't* want. So I instruct you, in carrying out my instructions which are not what you want but which are what I want, to tell yourself that: on the contrary, you are doing what you want and not what I want.

On top of all this, orders may not only be contradictory, incompatible, or disguised, they may be paradoxical. A paradoxical order is one which, if correctly executed, is disobeyed: if disobeyed, it is obeyed. Don't do what I tell you. Don't believe me. Be spontaneous.

I have been able to observe actual real-life family situations that embody all the above possibilities, and others.

The situation is complex, but once one begins to break some of the rules against seeing the rules, one realizes that much of one's difficulty is not due to the intrinsic complexity of the subject but to one's inhibitions against seeing what may be obvious, once the inhibition against seeing it is undone. There remain inhibitions against putting into words, such real or imagined insights.

[1]See especially *Pragmatics of Human Communication, A Study of Interactional Patterns, Pathologies, and Paradoxes.* Paul Watzlawick, Janet H. Beavin, and Don D. Jackson. W. N. Norton & Co. Inc., New York, 1967.

I have never come across a family that does not draw a line somewhere as to: *what may be put into words,* and, *what words what may be put into.* This is a problem that confronts us at this very minute.

• • •

If my view is right, there are many of you who are listening to me at this moment who do not know you have *rules against knowing about certain rules.*

Some of you sense that you have rules about rules but perhaps have never thought about it, in these terms.

Some of you are clear about all this. You shall have to bear with me, for a little, before I get to where you are at, if I can.

I want to talk a little about the rules that we cannot talk about – to talk just enough to convince any of you who are not sure what I am talking about, that I am talking about a very important issue, that I cannot talk about, more directly.

There is a law against murder. We can talk about murder, and about the law about murder.

There is a law against incest. We can talk about the law against incest, rather more freely than we can talk about incest: commonly there is a rule against talking about incest, in front of the children especially: but not an absolute rule against talking about whether or not there is a law against incest.

It used to be obvious to many (including Lévy-Bruhl) that when incest does not happen it is because there is a "natural" revulsion against it. To many, it may now seem equally obvious that it does not occur more frequently because there are rules against it.

Many people used to be scandalized by this view, for it seems to imply that if there were not such rules, people might do what was prohibited. Many people felt, and some no doubt still do, that to admit that there were rules against incest, would be to admit that parents and children, and brothers and sisters might *want* to have sexual relations with each other. Why should there be a rule against what no one "naturally" wants to do? Freud's view was that what people think they "naturally" don't want to do *may* be a product of repression, and other operations, at the behest of rules against even thinking much less doing it. The desire, even the thought, *and* the rule against the desire or thought, are all eliminated from our awareness, so that the product of these operations on oneself is a "normal" state of awareness, whereby one is unaware of the desire, the thought *and* the rules, and the operations.

One tends to assume that every negative rule (such as that against incest) implies a prior desire, impulse, propensity, instinct, tendency to do it. Don't do that, implies that one would be inclined to if not forbidden.

There is treasure at the bottom of the tree. You will find it. Only remember not to think of a white monkey. The moment you do, the treasure will be lost to you forever. (A favourite story of Francis Huxley.)

We can, by direct experiment verify that some negative injunctions have a paradoxical effect, to induce one to do what one has been told not to, *especially if one did not*, and does not, in fact, wish to.

"I would never have thought of it until I was told that I must not."

Negative rules may themselves generate actions they prohibit. If you want people not to do something, they are not doing, do not forbid it. There is a better chance that I will not think what I have not yet thought, if you do not tell me *not* to.

In this last minute, I have not been trying to establish whether or not incest is ruled out by social rules or natural law, or both. I have wished only to demonstrate that there is not a rule against talking *about* whether or not there are such rules or such a natural law.

A family has a rule that little Johnny should not think filthy thoughts. Little Johnny is a good boy: he does not have to be told not to think filthy thoughts. They never have *taught* him *not* to think filthy thoughts. He never has.

So, according to the family, and even little Johnny, there is no rule against filthy thoughts, because there is no need to have a rule against what never happens. Moreover, we do not talk in the family about a rule against filthy thoughts, because since there are no filthy thoughts, and no rule against them, there is no need to talk about this dreary, abstract, irrelevant or even vaguely filthy subject. There is no rule against talking about a non-existent rule about non-existent filthy thoughts: and no rule against talking about non-existent talk about a non-existent rule about something that is non-existent.

Probably no one outside of that particular family system would "buy" all that. But we probably all know *other* families who sell this sort of thing to themselves.

Rule A: Don't. Rule A.1.: Rule A does not exist. Rule A.2.: Do not discuss the existence of non-existence of Rules A, A.1, or A.2.

This type of ruling applies only to some rules. One can talk about certain rules (when one can cross the street). But there are certain rules that one cannot talk about without breaking the rule that one should not talk about them.

If you obey these rules, you will not know that they exist. There is no rule against talking about putting one's finger into one's own mouth, one's brother's, sister's, mother's, father's, anyone's mouth. No rule against *talking* about putting one's finger into the custard pie, though there *is* a rule about putting one's finger into the custard pie. No rule against recognizing the rule: don't put your finger into the fire. Why not? Because you will burn yourself. There is no rule against *talking* about it and giving reasons for it.

But, I may say, I have never put my finger a number of . . . (unmentionable) places?[2] What places? I can't mention them. Why not? I can't say.

One cannot talk about a rule about which one cannot talk. We have reached a limit to what we can talk about.

•   •   •

I have thought about the problem of how not to think a thought one is not supposed to think. I cannot think of any way to do so except, in some peculiar way, to "think" what one must not think in order to ensure that one does not think it.

"Of course", it never would even occur to a perfectly brainwashed person to think certain un-mentionably filthy thoughts. Such cleanliness, however, requires constant vigilance: vigilance against what? The answer is strictly unthinkable. To have clean

[2]"Unmentionable" only in relation to what cannot be related to it, (my finger) in this particular context.

memories, reveries, desires, dreams, imagination, one must keep clean company, and guard all senses against pollution. If one only overhears someone else talking filthy, one has been polluted. Even if one can forget one ever heard it, right away. But one has to remember to continue to forget and remember to remember to avoid that person in future.

Many such rules about rules apply to what parts of whose body can be "thought" of in relation to whom.

Rules apply to what kinds of sensations one is supposed to have where and when in one's own body, in relation to whom.

What are the funny places where funny feelings go on? Where do they come from? Where do they go to?

One seeks to avoid painful feelings, but there are many pleasureable feelings many people are forbidden to experience, imagine, remember, dream about, and definitely forbidden to talk about the fact that they are forbidden to talk about them. This is easy if one has already obeyed the injunction not even to "think" of what I can possibly be talking about.

One has then got to the position in which one cannot think *that* one cannot think about what one cannot think about because there is a rule against thinking about the X, and a rule against thinking that there is a rule against thinking that one must *not* think about *not* thinking about certain things.

If certain things cannot be thought about: and among the certain things that cannot be thought, is that there are certain things that cannot be thought, including the aforementioned thought, then: he who had complied with this calculus of anti-thoughts will not be aware he is not aware that he is obeying a rule not to think that he is obeying a rule not to think about X. So he is not aware of X and not aware he is not aware of the rule against being not aware of X. By obeying a rule not to realize he is obeying a rule, he will deny that there is any rule he is obeying.

Last week I began to look at a little of the structure of one of the varieties of the Western "conscience". One admires its ingenuity. It must constitute one of the biggest knots in which man has ever tied himself. One of its many peculiar features is that the more tied in the knot, the less aware are we that we are tied in it.

•   •   •

Anyone fully caught in the full anti-calculus of this kind cannot possibly avoid being bad in order to be good. In order to comply with the rules, rules have to be broken. Even if one could wash out one's brain three times a day, part of one's self must be aware of what one is not supposed to know in order to assure the continuance of those paradoxical states of multiplex ignorance, spun in the paradoxical spiral that the more we comply with the law, the more we break the law: the more righteous we become the deeper in sin: our *righteousness* is as filthy rags.

I alluded in particular last week to rules governing projection, as a mapping of a set of attributions within our family, onto the social cosmos outside the family.

In this last talk I want to draw your attention briefly to the converse operation to projection, namely, introjection.

Both can be thought of as mapping operations, whereby elements and relations between elements, from one set, called the domain, are mapped onto elements and relations between elements called a range.

There can be many different mappings from one set into another. There can be mappings of one set into itself.

If ϕ is a mapping of A into B, set A is called the domain of ϕ, and set B the range of ϕ.

Projection can then be regarded as a mapping of inside onto outside, and introjection a mapping of outside into inside. Families are of peculiar significance and interest because, more than any other social set, they are both domain and range, for projections *to* outside, introjections *from* outside into them; *and*, they are the range for *projections* onto them *from* the members of the family itself, as they are the domain of introjections onto individuals in the family. Projections onto the family, from family members, combined with introjections onto them from outside, are combined to form a product which is in turn further projected and introjected: such projections and introjections are in turn introjected and projected, and so on, endlessly.

One's body is of unique significance because it is *the* range for "introjective" mappings from all domains: and these introjective sets provide a "pool" for projections in turn *to* any domain, from which reintrojections and re-reprojections and re-re-projections and re-re-re-introjections, can be, and *are,* carried on, possibly without end. However, in practice the contingency possibilities are restricted considerably, as we know, of *what* may be mapped onto *what.* This we shall have to examine.

The family supplies the principal *domain* from which introjective ϕ maps are made. The *nexification* of the family[3] is the intensive mapping again and again of $F \rightarrow F \rightarrow F \rightarrow F \ldots$ within the sets and subsets of the network of whole person and part-object familial relations, over generations.

•   •   •

The family is also the *range* for introjective mappings *from* domains outside the family. These family introjections are the domain from which the baby and infant is subject to phantasization. The infant is the *final common range*, as it were, – where all introjections converge and permutate, are pooled and stored to become a sort of ϕ *bank*[4], the subsequent *domain, from* which

[3]Adumbrated by me in "Individual and Family Structure". In Lomas, P. (Ed.), *The Predicament of the Family.* Hogarth Press, London, 1967.
[4]See *Self and Others.* R. D. Laing. Tavistock: London; Pantheon: New York.

subsequent projections will be released (according to some curious chronometer whose nature we have yet to determine), to find *their range*, anywhere from a marital relation, a nuclear family, a social network, to the *total social world system*, or even the total cosmos.

The social world system as range, with its subsets already multiply mapped by projections, becomes in turn the domain from which, through the family, introjective mappings are concentrated, once more to be reprojected. . . .

One should in no way be deterred by difference of magnitude between domain and range. One can project a minute domain onto a vast range; or a vast domain onto a minute range. *Scale* is no deterrent in practice. (cf., astrology, palmistry, alchemical medicine; man, the microcosm, as "image" of macrocosm: possible analogy with holograms, and so on.) It is not a question of the "scientific" truth, or value, of such mappings. We are however in the true realm of science when we study what these mappings are. They exist no less today as before. But they are very inadequately studied "scientifically", whether by psychologists or sociologists, or anthropologists, when it comes to "ourselves" rather than "primitive" societies.[5]

The operation whereby this mapping is done, is usually "unconscious". People describe what is an image of an image of an image, but they do not realize that this is what it is, taking it instead to be some sort of primary reality.

In order to develop this theory further, we would need to make an incursion into the mathematical theory of mapping, and this must be deferred for another time.

The set of relations *in* which we were to begin with, is the refractive medium through which in the modality of phantasy (ϕ), we experience the world as a projection of ourselves, and ourselves in terms of the introjection by us of the shared image of the world our particular culture(s) transmits.

It is always human agents who are projecting and introjecting.

Suppose I project my mother onto my wife. She takes on the ϕ-value of my mother *for me*. That is projection. However (cf., Ch. 2) I may or may not *induce* her to embody my mother. The

[5]"The Head and the Loins: Levi-Strauss and Beyond." R. G. Willis. *Man*, No. 4, Dec., 1967, pp. 518-534.

operation of inducing her to embody my projection is what I am calling *induction*. Projection is done by one person as his *own* experience, of the other. *Induction* is done by one person to *the other's* experience. We have actually no word for the transformation of the *other's* experience under such induction. Introjection is an operation *by* me on *my* experience, which is identical in principle with projection, the only difference being that the locations of the transference are different, namely: from any region of what is taken to be not-me, or not-self, or not that with which I identify myself (e.g., my family), on*to* what I take to be "me", "self", or that with which I identify myself.

It is not sufficient to say that my wife introjects my mother, if by projection, and induction, I have manoeuvred her into such a position that she actually begins to act, and even to feel, like her. She may begin to act and feel like her without ever having met her. Indeed, it is quite possible for my actions to induce another to feel and act like someone I myself may never have known.

Let us take a fictitious example in which I shall use the first person only for simplicity. My father lost his mother when he was a boy and was brought up by his older sister. His wife was rather a big sister – cum mother – to him. He never had a daughter, and I knew he missed one. When I get married he finds in my wife the mother he lost, and this fits her own image of herself derived from her mother and father. By this convergence of projections upon her, she is finally induced to be more than a mere image for such projections: she becomes the very embodiment of someone (or of an amalgam of persons) she has never met, or even hardly heard of. Having been induced to become my father's mother, whom does that tend to induce me into? My son into? My daughter into? And so on.

Such inductions are going on, in my view, all the time. All our action and reactions to the other, imply some coefficient of induction. We very seldom ever entirely relate absolutely accurately to the other. And indeed very seldom is there an other there to whom one could. We make a gesture, that is itself an induced embodiment of an image of another *of* another projected upon oneself by another; this gesture in turn induces more or less compellingly from the other to whom we address it a complementary gesture; this last gesture induced by my induced gesture, induces in *me* in turn a gesture that responds by a further induction . . . and so the play goes on.

•   •   •

I have tried to reveal a state which becomes more so the less it is recognized.

This is a difficult state to live through. We are prepared to be happy, or unhappy, satisfied or frustrated, hopeful or despairing, good or evil. As long as we know where we are: as long as we feel orientated. We think we know *where*, what, when, who, even how and why we are.

We would rather be anywhere, as long as we are somewhere. We would rather be anyone, as long as we are someone.

We can *cling* to being a Christian, a married man, a housewife, a dutiful daughter, to attributions, even unpleasant ones. But *we*, by the very fact that we "cling" to such identities, testify in the very act of so doing, that *we* who are clinging, are not that to which we cling.

Our family of origin has done its best. It has given us its range of distinctions, options, identities, definitions, rules, repertoires of operations, instructions, attributions, loci, scenarios, roles, parts to play. . . .

But it has not told us, who are "we" who play those parts and take up those positions. That is the question.

Some of you may feel that I have recklessly generalized from particular instances of "pathology", to the "normal". Since I have met hardly any of you who may hear or read this, I must leave you to take or leave what you may find in what I've said that may seem interesting or relevant to you. Here is one last example, which I offer to suggest that the gap between what seems to be abnormal or deviant or pathological, and what does not, may be more superficial than it appears at first encounter. This is a conversation between a mother and her 14-year-old daughter.

M (to 14-year-old daughter): You are evil.
D: No, I'm not.
M: Yes, you are.
D: Uncle Jack doesn't think so.

M: He doesn't love you as I do. Only a mother really knows the truth about her daughter, and only one who loves you as I do will ever tell you the truth about yourself no matter what it is. If you don't believe me, just look at yourself in the mirror[6] carefully and you will see that I'm telling the truth.

The daughter did and saw that her mother was right after all, and realized how wrong she had been not to be grateful for having a mother who so loved her that she would tell her the truth about herself. Whatever it might be.

This example may appear somewhat disturbing, even sinister. Suppose we changed one word in it: replace "evil" by "pretty".

M: You are pretty.
D: No, I'm not.
M: Yes, you are.
D: Uncle Jack doesn't think so.
M: He doesn't love you as I do. Only a mother really knows the truth about her daughter, and only one who loves you as I do will ever tell you the truth about yourself no matter what it is. If you don't believe me, just look at yourself in the mirror carefully, and you will see that I'm telling you the truth.

The *technique* is exactly the same. Whether the attribution is pretty, good, beautiful, ugly, or evil, the *structure* is identical. The structure is *so* common that we hardly notice it unless the attribution jars. We all employ some recognizably similar version of this technique and may be prepared to justify it. I suggest that we meditate upon the *structure* of the *induction,* not only the *content* thereof.

What, I think, we find most immediately disturbing about this can be expressed in general terms as follows: the other person induces self to map into self's own image of self a value which, we feel, should not be mapped onto self; the self-system is a range that should not, we may feel, be mapped in that way, in any circumstances or only under extreme circumstances.

Nevertheless, if it was another value we felt to be more "ap-

[6] Compare: Winnicott, D. W. "Mirror-role of Mother and Family in Child Development". In *The Predicament of the Family,* 1967, op. cit.
And: Lacan, Jacques. "Le Stade du miroir comme formateur de la fonction du Je". In *Écrits* Editions du Seuil, 1966.
Translation: "The Mirror-phase as formative of the function of the I". *New Left Review,* No. 51, 1968, pp. 71-77.

propriate", we might not feel disturbed. Further: if a child were taught to map the same value, "evil", onto a region regarded as the *proper* range for such a value in *essentially the same way*, that, also would not, I think, disturb us.

Hitler was an evil man, for example. We teach our children that, and many similar things, before they can possibly make up their own minds, from "the evidence". We may feel that someone is positively evil if he does *not* feel that Hitler was an evil man. Take racism: semitism; anti-semitism; anti-anti-semitism. Blacks and Whites. Black Anti-Whites. White Anti-Blacks. White trash and Niggers. "Anyone who thinks in that way is worse than they are." Black Anti-Anti-Whites. White Anti-Anti-Blacks. Even those of us who think we do not employ such values, tend still to use them but they are now reserved for those who employ them.

"I don't think the Whites are any more degenerate, essentially, than us Blacks. But anyone who talks about Niggers is really White trash."

"I don't think the Whites are superior to the Blacks, essentially, but those Blacks who incite violence and talk about 'White monkeys', are no better than monkeys themselves."

As long as we cannot up-level our "thinking" beyond Us and Them, the goodies and baddies, it will go on and on. The only possible end will be when all the goodies have killed all the baddies, and all the baddies all the goodies, which does not seem so difficult or unlikely since to Us, we are the goodies and They are the baddies, while to Them, we are the baddies and they are the goodies.

Millions of people have died this century and millions more are going to, including, we have every reason to expect, many of Us and our children, because we cannot break this knot.

It seems a comparatively simple knot, but it is tied *very, very* tight – round the throat, as it were, of the whole human species.

But don't believe me because I say so, look in the mirror and see for yourself.